A Prayer Coloring Book

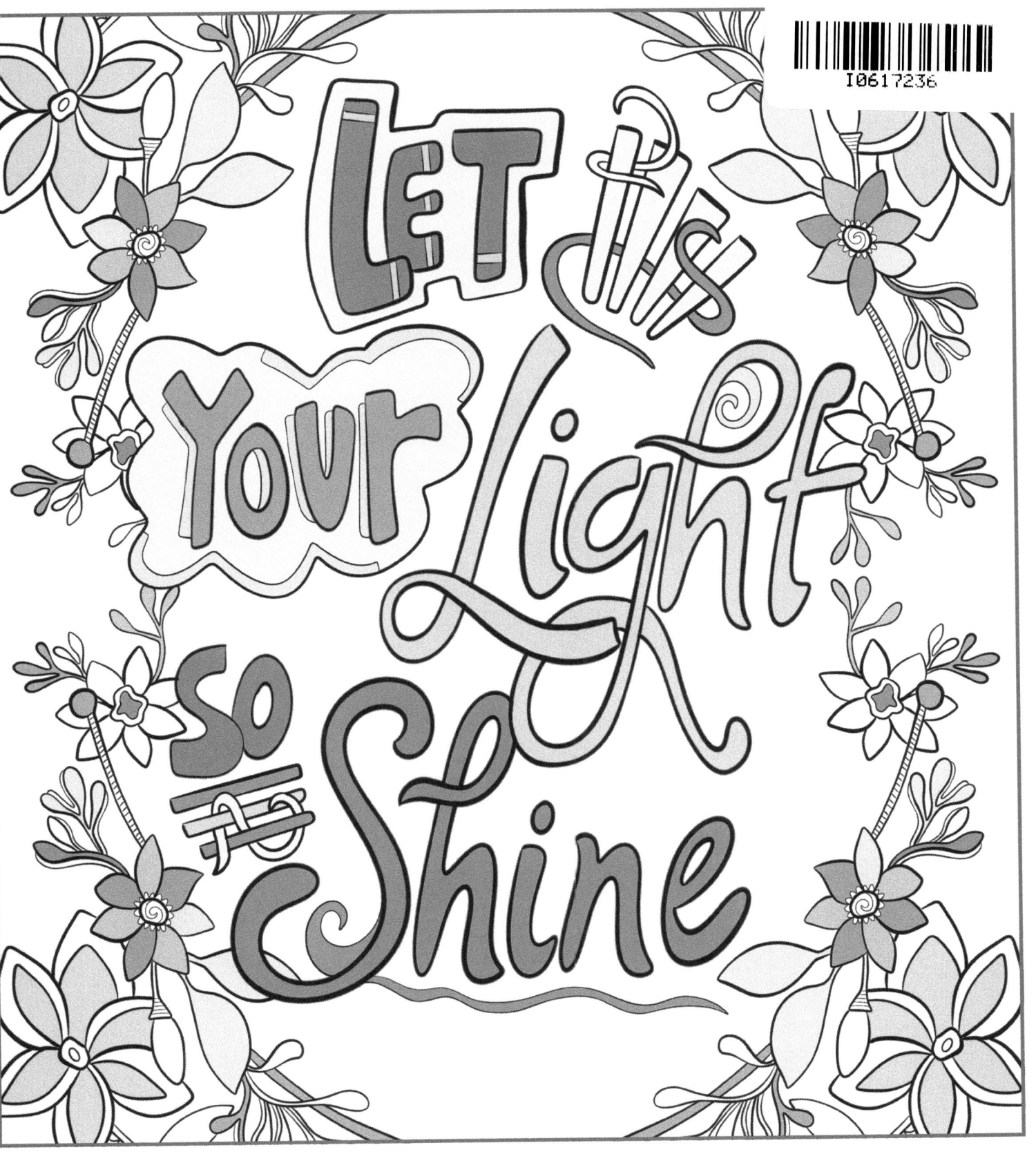

Let Your Light So Shine

Samantha Snyder

Doodle Art Alley Books

Let Your Light So Shine: A Prayer Coloring Book is available
at special discounts when purchased in quantities for
educational use, fundraising, or sales promotions.
For more information, contact: info@akabooks.com

Scripture quotations are taken from the
Holy Bible, King James Version (Public Domain).

Cover images © 2024 by Doodle Art Alley.

Cover and page design by Zaccarine Design, Inc.

ISBN: 979-8-9890357-0-0

This edition is published by aka Associates.
www.akabooks.com

DOODLE ART ALLEY BOOKS

This book belongs to:

_____

_____

_____

Pray hardest when it's Hardest to Pray

—Anonymous

Peace Prayer of St. Francis of Assisi

Lord, make me an instrument of your peace:
where there is hatred, let me sow love;
where there is injury, pardon;
where there is doubt, faith;
where there is despair, hope;
where there is darkness, light;
where there is sadness, joy.

O divine Master, grant that I may not so much seek
to be consoled as to console,
to be understood as to understand,
to be loved as to love.
For it is in giving that we receive,
it is in pardoning that we are pardoned,
and it is in dying that we are born to eternal life.
Amen.

PRAYER is the inner bath of Love into which the Soul plunges itself. St. John Vianney

Doodle Art Alley ©

"Give me faith, Lord, and let me help others find it."

Leo Tolstoy

Walk at dawn with a winged heart and give thanks for another day of loving.

Kahlil Gibran

Looking behind,
I am filled
with gratitude.
Looking forward,
I am filled
with vision.
Looking upwards,
I am filled
with strength.
Looking within,
I discover peace.

Apache Prayer

There Shall be Showers of blessing.

EZEKIEL 34:26

PRAYER is the mortar that holds our HOUSE together. Mother Teresa

The Wish to Pray is a prayer in itself.

Georges Bernanos

The Lord's Prayer

Our Father which art in heaven,
Hallowed be thy name.
Thy kingdom come.
Thy will be done in earth, as *it is* in heaven.
Give us this day our daily bread.
And forgive us our debts,
as we forgive our debtors.
And lead us not into temptation,
but deliver us from evil:
For thine is the kingdom,
and the power, and the glory, for ever.
Amen.
Matthew 6:9-13

1 Corinthians 16:14

If the only prayer you said in your whole life was, "THANK YOU" that would suffice.

Meister Eckhart

The Lord is my Shepherd; I shall not want. He maketh me to lie down in green pastures: He leadeth me beside the Still waters. He Restoreth my Soul.

Psalm 23:1-3

May the road rise
up to meet you.
May the wind be
always at your back.
May the sun shine
warm upon your face;
the rains fall soft
upon your fields
and until we meet again,
may God hold you
in the palm of His hand.

Irish Blessing

Don't Pray When it RAINS if You don't Pray When The Sun Shines

Satchel Paige

For We Walk by FAITH, not by Sight.

2 Corinthians 5:7

Doodle Art Alley ©

In Prayer It is better to have a heart without words than words without a heart.

John Bunyan

May the earth
continue to live.
May the heavens above
continue to live.
May the rains
continue to dampen the land.
May the wet forests
continue to grow.
Then the flowers shall bloom
And we people shall live again.

Hawaiian Prayer

There are two ways of spreading *Light*: to be The Candle or the mirror that reflects it.

Edith Wharton

Ye are the Light of the World

Matthew 5:14

Doodle Art Alley ©

Rejoicing in HOPE; patient in tribulation; continuing instant in Prayer;

Romans 12:12

Doodle Art Alley ©

The value of persistent prayer is not that HE will hear us, but that WE will hear Him.

William McGill

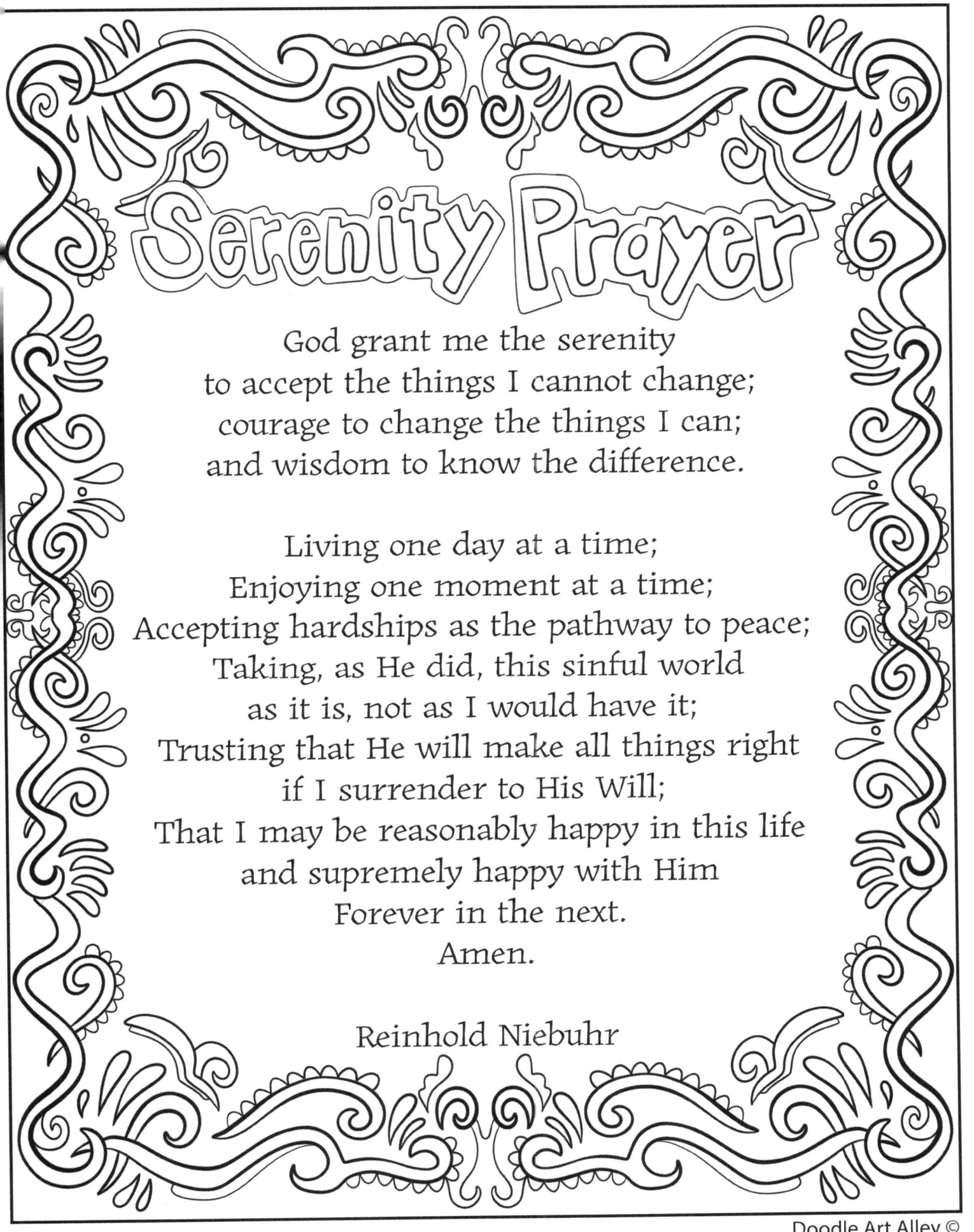

Serenity Prayer

God grant me the serenity
to accept the things I cannot change;
courage to change the things I can;
and wisdom to know the difference.

Living one day at a time;
Enjoying one moment at a time;
Accepting hardships as the pathway to peace;
Taking, as He did, this sinful world
as it is, not as I would have it;
Trusting that He will make all things right
if I surrender to His Will;
That I may be reasonably happy in this life
and supremely happy with Him
Forever in the next.
Amen.

Reinhold Niebuhr

I SEE THE Moon, and the Moon SEES ME. GOD bless the Moon, and GOD bless ME.

- Nursery Rhyme

Doodle Art Alley ©

Doodle Art Alley ©

prayer should be the key of the day and the lock of the night.

George Herbert

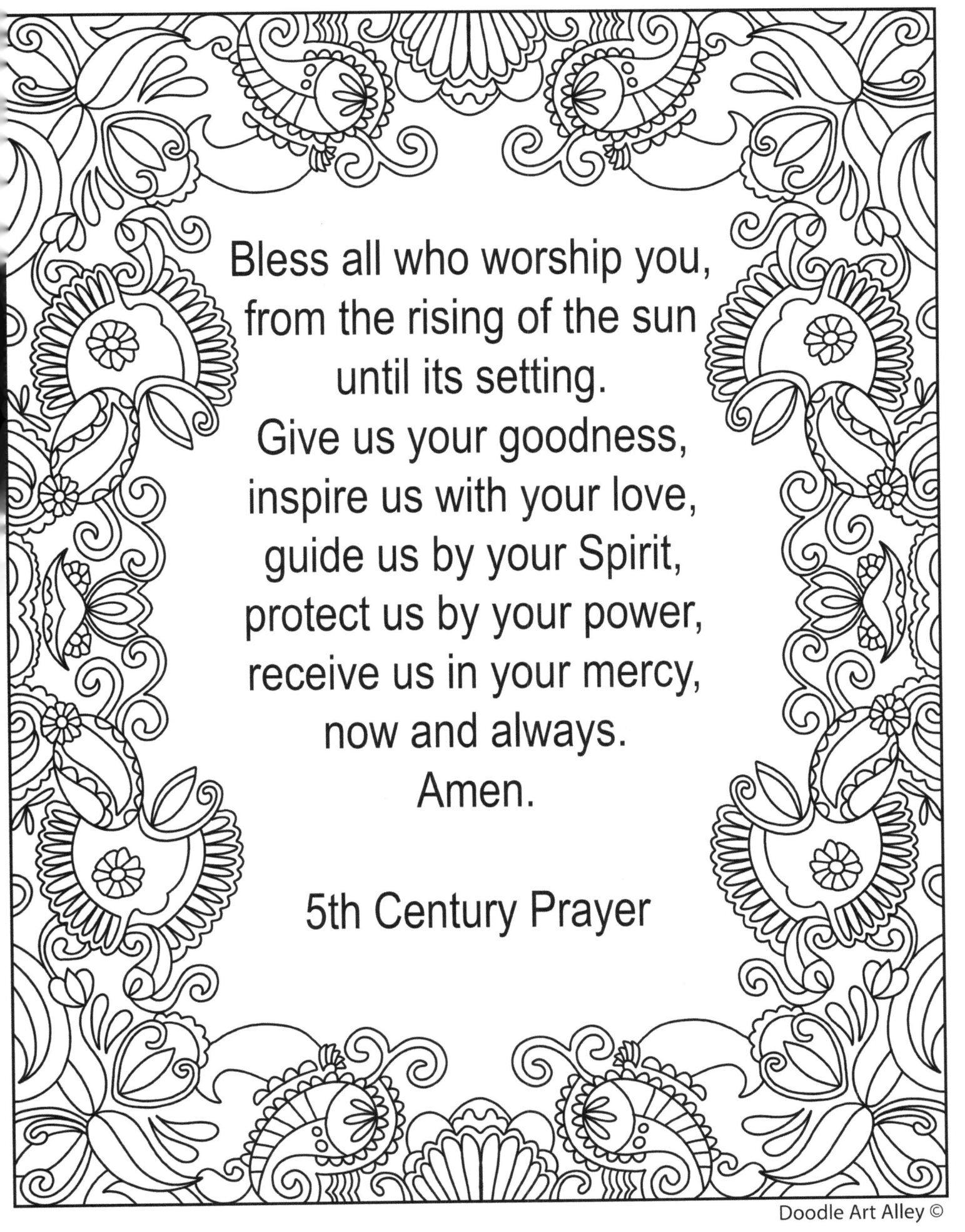

Bless all who worship you,
from the rising of the sun
until its setting.
Give us your goodness,
inspire us with your love,
guide us by your Spirit,
protect us by your power,
receive us in your mercy,
now and always.
Amen.

5th Century Prayer

Behold, I send an Angel before thee, Exodus 23:20

God speaks in the silence of the heart. Listening is the beginning of prayer.

Mother Teresa

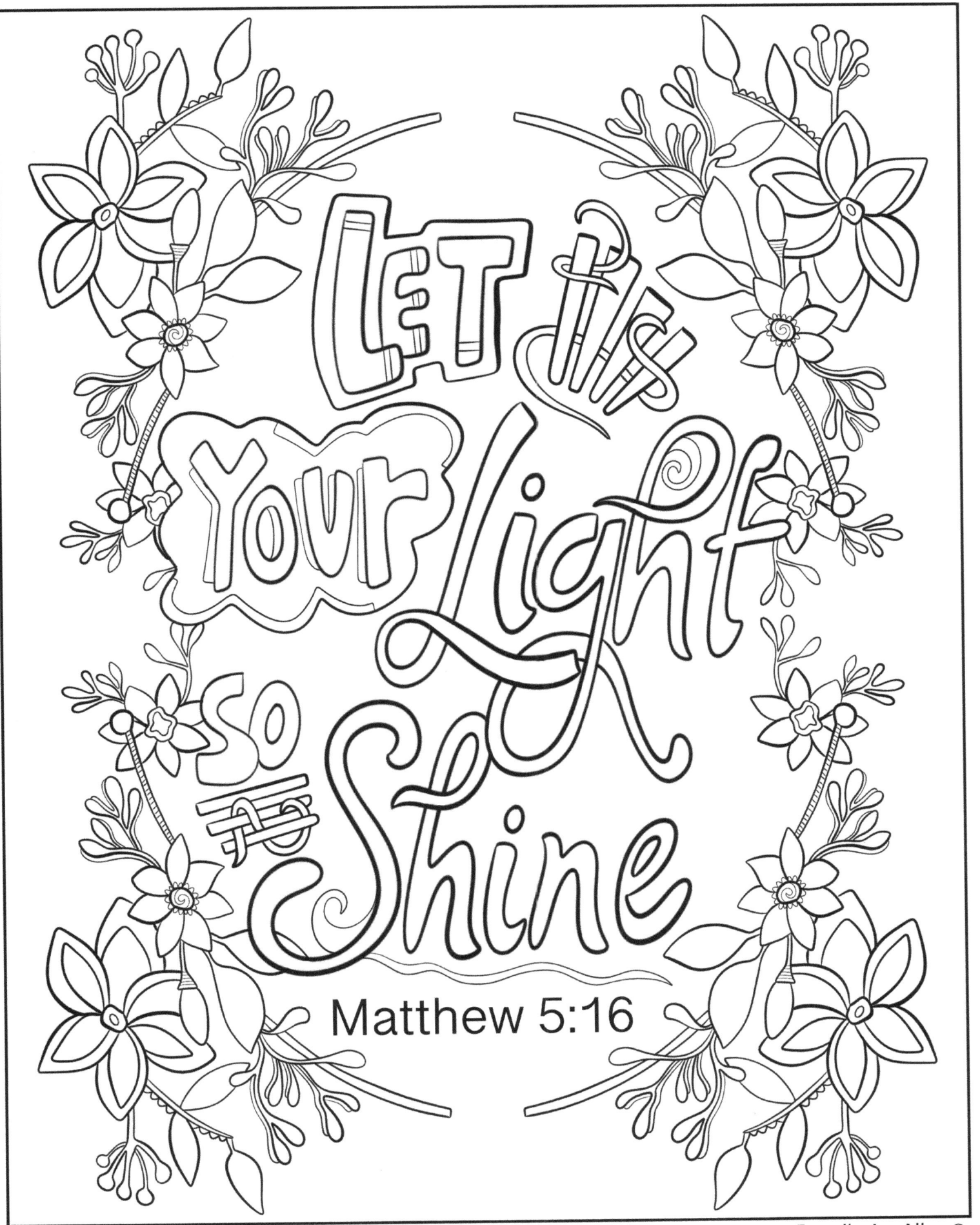

Let His Your Light So Shine

Matthew 5:16

Although the people living
across the ocean surrounding us,
I believe, are all our
brothers and sisters,
why are there constant troubles
in our world?
Why do winds and waves rise
in the ocean surrounding us?
I only earnestly wish that the wind
will soon puff away all the clouds
which are hanging over
the tops of the mountains.

Shinto Prayer

PRAY WITHOUT CEASING.

1 Thessalonians 5:17

Walk as children of Light

Ephesians 5:8

This is the day which the **Lord** hath made; we will **rejoice** and be glad in it. Psalm 118:24

Doodle Art Alley ©

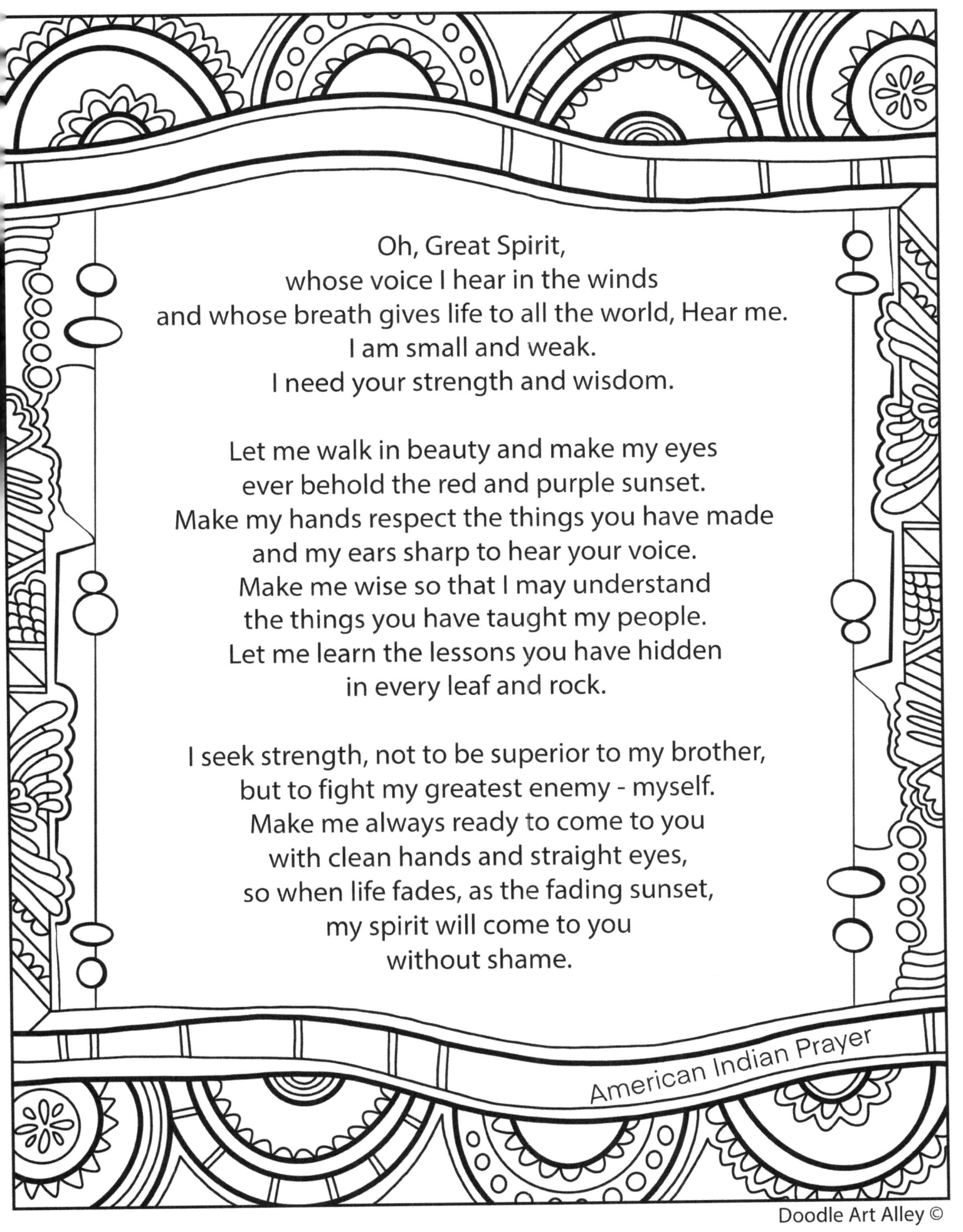

Oh, Great Spirit,
whose voice I hear in the winds
and whose breath gives life to all the world, Hear me.
I am small and weak.
I need your strength and wisdom.

Let me walk in beauty and make my eyes
ever behold the red and purple sunset.
Make my hands respect the things you have made
and my ears sharp to hear your voice.
Make me wise so that I may understand
the things you have taught my people.
Let me learn the lessons you have hidden
in every leaf and rock.

I seek strength, not to be superior to my brother,
but to fight my greatest enemy - myself.
Make me always ready to come to you
with clean hands and straight eyes,
so when life fades, as the fading sunset,
my spirit will come to you
without shame.

American Indian Prayer

Doodle Art Alley ©

Love your enemies, bless them that curse you.

Matthew 5:44

Doodle Art Alley ©

Be Strong and Courageous

2 Chronicles 32:7

Doodle Art Alley ©

Dear Father, hear and bless Thy beasts and singing birds. And guard with tenderness Small things that have no words.

Child's Prayer

Doodle Art Alley ©

May there always be work
for your hands to do.
May your purse always hold
a coin or two.
May the sun always shine
upon your window pane.
May a rainbow be certain
to follow each rain.
May the hand of a friend
always be near to you and
May God fill your heart
with gladness to cheer you.

Irish Blessing

I do not ask to walk smooth paths
Nor bear an easy load.
I pray for strength and fortitude
To climb the rock strewn road.

Give me courage and I can scale
The hardest peaks alone,
And transform every stumbling block
Into a stepping stone.

Gail Brook Burket

Doodle Art Alley ©

Any concern too small to be turned into a **Prayer** is too small to be made into a burden.

Corrie Ten Boom

Doodle Art Alley ©

Pray as though everything depended on GOD. Work as though everything depended on YOU.

St. Augustine

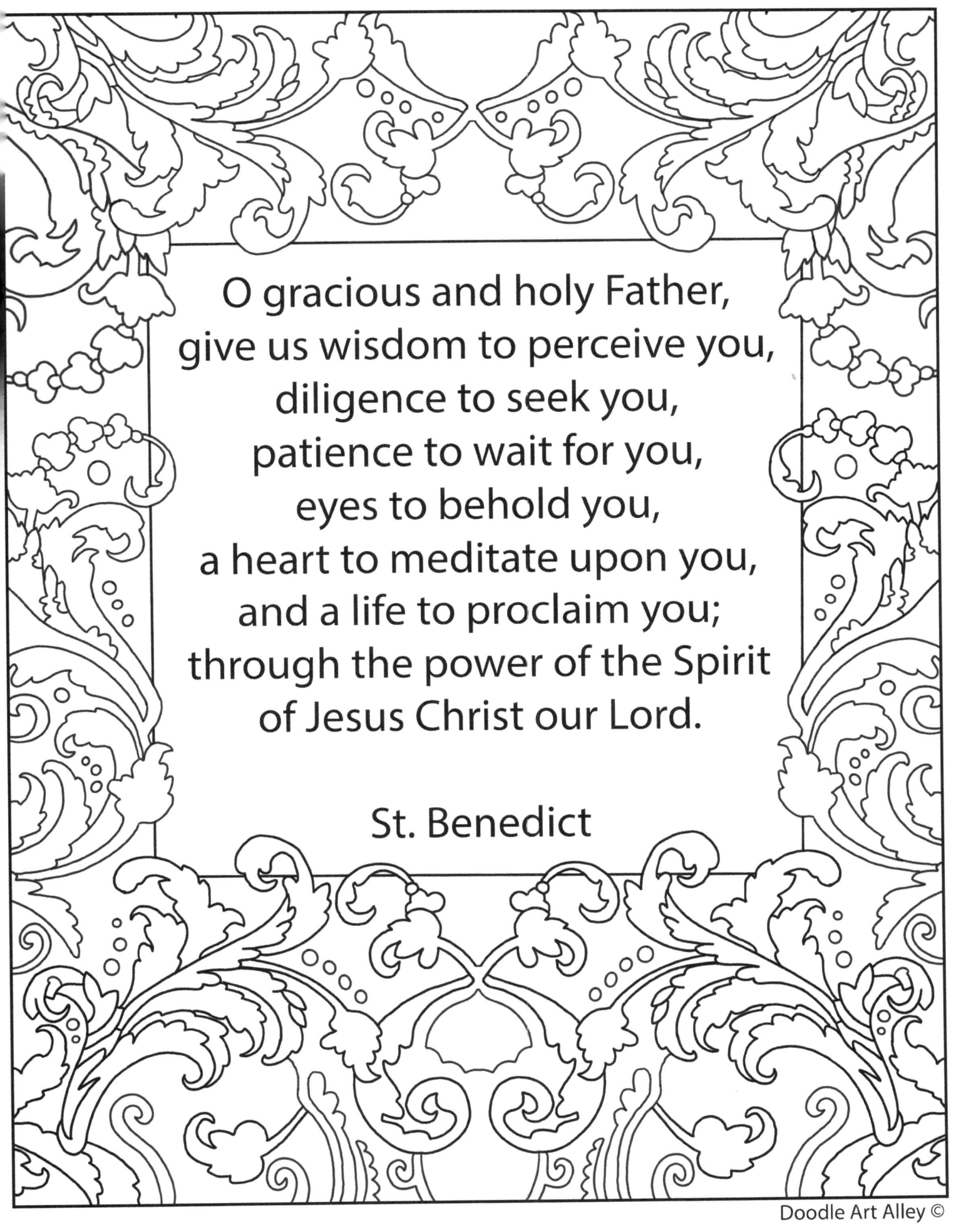

O gracious and holy Father,
give us wisdom to perceive you,
diligence to seek you,
patience to wait for you,
eyes to behold you,
a heart to meditate upon you,
and a life to proclaim you;
through the power of the Spirit
of Jesus Christ our Lord.

St. Benedict

Doodle Art Alley ©

Set Your Affection on things Above.

Colossians 3:2

True Beauty Begins Inside

unknown

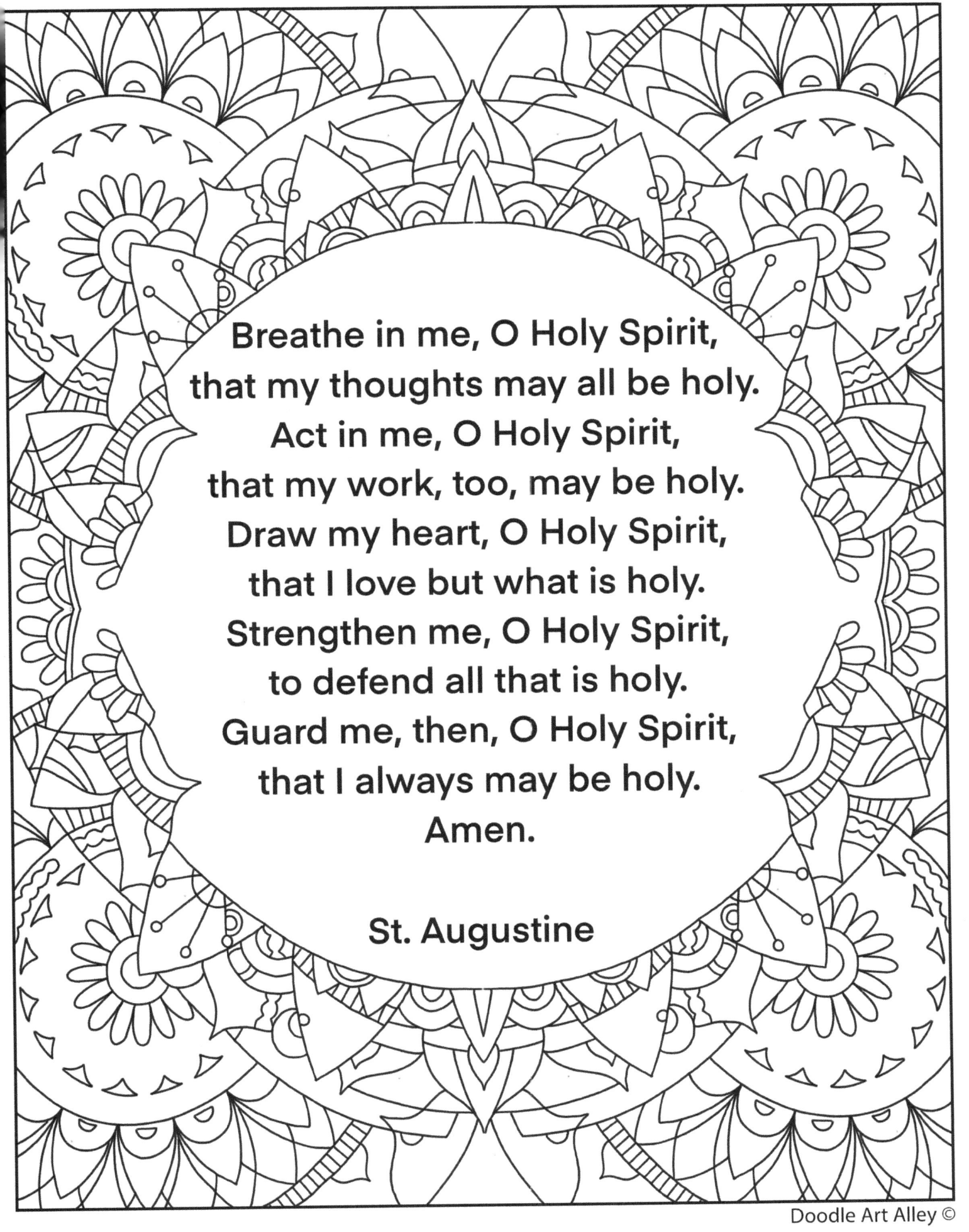

Breathe in me, O Holy Spirit,
that my thoughts may all be holy.
Act in me, O Holy Spirit,
that my work, too, may be holy.
Draw my heart, O Holy Spirit,
that I love but what is holy.
Strengthen me, O Holy Spirit,
to defend all that is holy.
Guard me, then, O Holy Spirit,
that I always may be holy.
Amen.

St. Augustine

You whose Day it is Make it Beautiful. Get out your Rainbow Colors So it will be Beautiful.

Nootka Indian Song

Doodle Art Alley ©

Prayer is not asking. It is a longing of the soul

Mahatma Gandhi

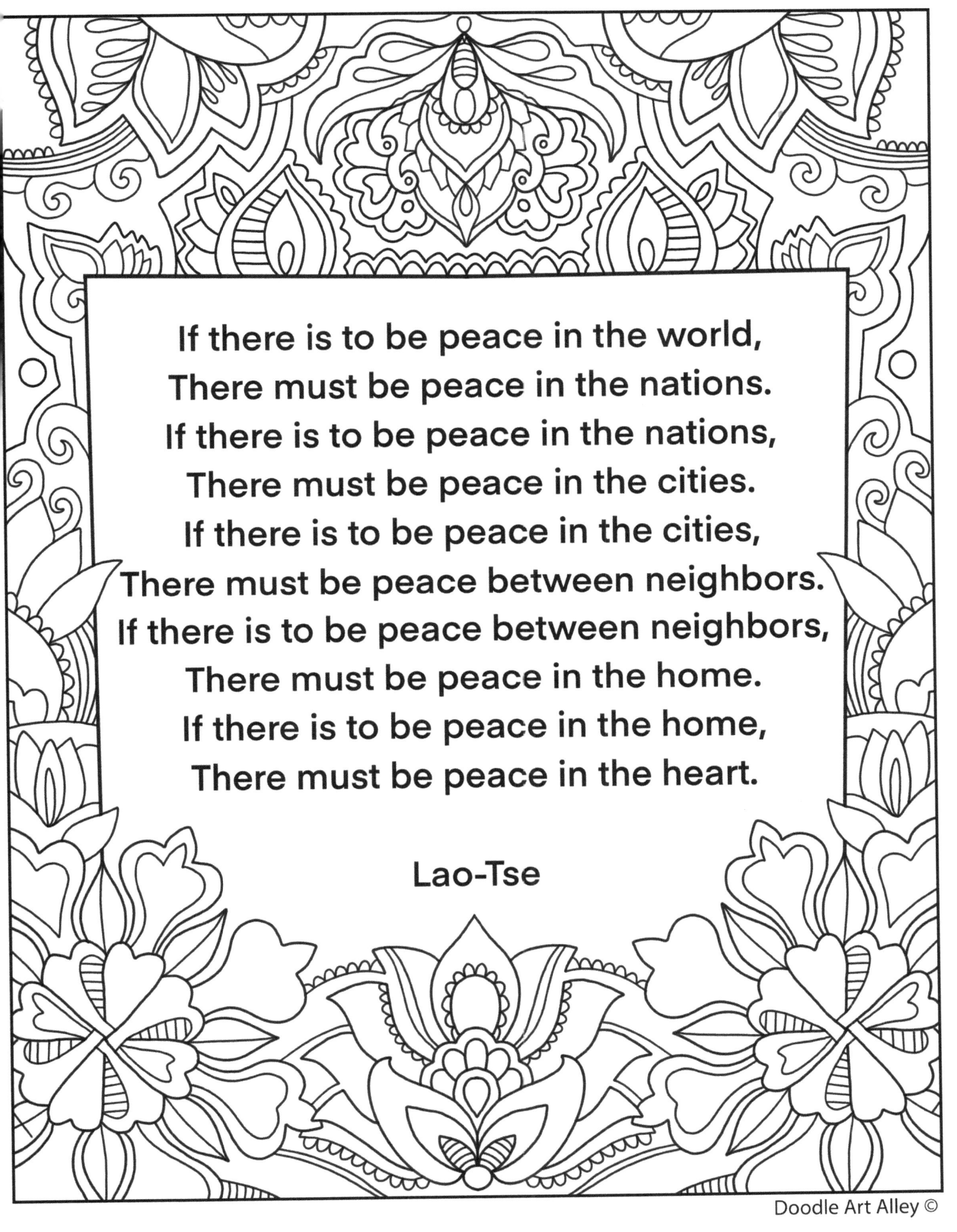

If there is to be peace in the world,
There must be peace in the nations.
If there is to be peace in the nations,
There must be peace in the cities.
If there is to be peace in the cities,
There must be peace between neighbors.
If there is to be peace between neighbors,
There must be peace in the home.
If there is to be peace in the home,
There must be peace in the heart.

Lao-Tse

Now I lay me Down to Sleep, I Pray the Lord my Soul to keep

Anonymous

ABOUT DOODLE ART ALLEY

Samantha Snyder is an award-winning artist. She is the creator of more than 25 best-selling books in the Doodle Art Alley Books series. Her books have earned the prestigious Mom's Choice Award®.

She has been doodling her whole life. While teaching elementary school, she often drew up coloring pages and printables for her students and fellow teachers. She decided to start sharing her creations and in 2008, Doodle Art Alley was founded.

A quick glance at a doodle may show scribbles, random lines and shapes with no meaning or significance. However, with a little love and direction, these drawings have the potential to compete with some of the best artwork there is!

Doodle Art Alley is dedicated to giving those squiggly lines the proper credit they deserve. Who would have thought that such a small and simple idea could possess so much potential?

There are lots of fun doodle art activities, tips, and information to read through and enjoy. Visit **www.doodle-art-alley.com** for hundreds of exciting doodles.

DOODLE ART ALLEY BOOKS

DOODLE ART ALLEY BOOKS

Samantha Snyder